Dams

By Virginia Loh-Hagan

21st Century
Junior Library

Published in the United States of America by
Cherry Lake Publishing
Ann Arbor, Michigan
www.cherrylakepublishing.com

Content Adviser: Dr. Todd Kelley, Associate Professor of Engineering/Technology Teacher Education, Purdue Polytechnic Institute, West Lafayette, Indiana
Reading Adviser: Marla Conn MS, Ed., Literacy specialist, Read-Ability, Inc.

Photo Credits: © Alex Papp/Shutterstock Images, cover; © Johnny Adolphson/Shutterstock Images, 4; © Charles Knowles/Shutterstock Images, 6; © curtis/Shutterstock Images, 8; © National Geographic Creative/Alamy Stock Photo, 10; © SF photo/Shutterstock Images, 12; © All Canada Photos/Alamy Stock Photo, 14; © turtix/Shutterstock Images, 16; © shutterlk/Shutterstock Images, 18

Library of Congress Cataloging-in-Publication Data
Names: Loh-Hagan, Virginia, author.
Title: Dams / by Virginia Loh-Hagan.
Description: Ann Arbor : Cherry Lake Publishing, [2017] | Series: 21st century junior library. Extraordinary engineering |
    Audience: K to grade 3. | Includes bibliographical references and index.
Identifiers: LCCN 2016032401| ISBN 9781634721639 (hardcover) | ISBN 9781634722957 (pbk.) |
    ISBN 9781634722292 (pdf) | ISBN 9781634723619 (ebook)
Subjects: LCSH: Dams—Juvenile literature. | Dams—Design and construction—Juvenile literature.
Classification: LCC TC540 .L64 2017 | DDC 627/.8—dc23
LC record available at https://lccn.loc.gov/2016032401

Cherry Lake Publishing would like to acknowledge the work of The Partnership for 21st Century Learning.
Please visit *www.p21.org* for more information.

Printed in the United States of America
Corporate Graphics

CONTENTS

The top of a dam is called a crest.

What Are Dams?

Dams are human-designed barriers. They stop water flow. They control water flow. They support the water behind them. Water pushes on dams. This **force** is called **pressure**. The pressure is greater at the bottom. So, engineers build dams in a triangle shape to hold the pressure. Dams have thick bottoms and thinner tops. Engineers solve problems by thinking of many things. Dams must be strong. They must be **waterproof**.

Most dams have spillways. They let water flow through.

Dams are built across streams or rivers. They're often built in **canyons**. They create a large pool of water. This pool is called a **reservoir**. It stores water. Water can be used for farming. It can be used for drinking. It can be used to create power. It can be used for fun. Dams also stop flooding. They can be helpful.

Think!

Think about why some people don't like dams. Read about the disadvantages of dams. Do you agree or disagree?

Broken dams follow the force of water.

How Do Buttresses Push Back on Water?

Water weighs a lot. It pushes forces against dams. Dams must push back with equal force. They must **redirect** the water's force. They push it into the ground where it can support the load. They push it into canyon walls.

Engineers design dams to firmly connect to the ground. This helps **resist** forces. Sometimes, the ground isn't strong enough. Engineers must make solid **foundations**.

The Daniel-Johnson Dam in Canada is a buttress dam made of concrete.

Buttress dams are a design option. These dams have walls supported by several buttresses. They're beams. They add more weight to dams. They **anchor** and brace dams. They're spaced apart. They're placed on the opposite side of the water. They push the water's forces to the ground. They stop dams from tipping over. They hold dams in place.

Look!

Look at a local dam. Where is it located? How big is it? What materials is it made of? What type is it?

Gravity dams, like the one at the Robert Moses Niagara Hydroelectric Power Station, need strong foundations.

How Does Gravity Push Back on Water?

Gravity dams are made of concrete. They're the largest dams. They're the heaviest dams. They're the highest dams. They have large bases. Their weight holds back water. It also resists water's forces. It pushes forces down to the ground. This means these dams use their gravity. Gravity is a strong force. It pushes weight downward.

The Gardiner Dam in Canada is one of the world's largest embankment dams.

Embankment dams are a type of gravity dam. But they're made from rock and earth. They're made from materials near their sites. Their walls match the natural slope of nature. They have a cover of clay or concrete. This cover stops leaks coming through the gaps in rocks. Embankment dams are very thick. They have large bases. They're heavy. Their weight resists water's forces.

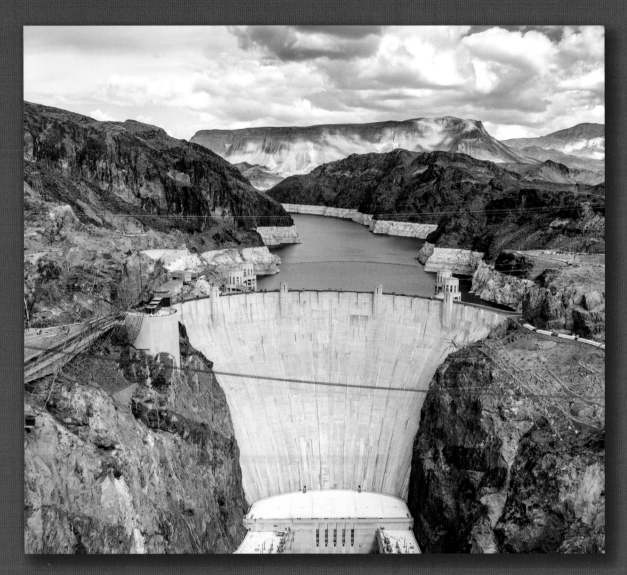

The Hoover Dam sits in the Black Canyon between Nevada and Arizona.

How Do Arches Push Back on Water?

Arch dams are in narrow canyons. Canyon walls support arch dams. **Notches** are cut into the walls. Arch dams are built to fit in the notches. They're built in a curved arch. Arches face the water. Their curved shape holds back water. It redirects water's forces into the walls. Water's forces are evenly spread out. No one area takes all the pressure.

Arch dams take advantage of water's forces.

Arch dams are thinner than other dams. They don't need the heavy weight. They use the canyon walls. They also use water's forces. Water pushes against the concrete. Arch dams squeeze together. This closes any gaps. This makes arch dams strong.

Ask Questions!

Ask parents or friends if they've visited a dam. Ask about their experience. Were they impressed? Would they visit again? Why or why not?

Try This!

Materials

extra-large aluminum baking pan, 2 buckets of sand, 2 buckets of pebbles, packet of popsicle sticks, cheesecloth, water

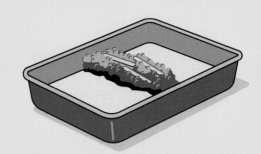

Procedures

1 Challenge yourself to make a dam. Use only listed materials.

2 Work outside. This activity can get messy.

3 Place pan on flat surface. Use the sand, pebbles, cheesecloth, and popsicle sticks to build a dam across the middle. Make the dam strong. Make sure it blocks water. Make sure water can't leak out. (Little leaks are okay.)

4 Test your dam. Add water to one side of the pan. What happens? Does the dam hold back water? Does it form a pool? Does it fall down? If so, rebuild. Then, retest.

Principle at Play

This activity shows how to build dams. Engineers think of several things. Dams must be strong. They must be waterproof. They must hold back water. They must hold in water. How can you improve your dam design? Use different materials. Add more water. Add pressure.

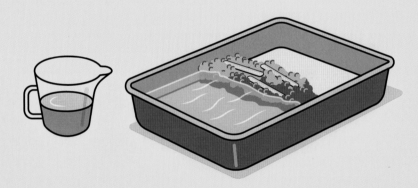

GLOSSARY

anchor (ANG-kur) to hold firmly in place in the ground

arch (AHRCH) curve

buttress (BUHT-ris) beam used as support

canyons (KAN-yuhnz) deep gorges with rivers or streams flowing through

embankment (em-BANGK-muhnt) raised structure used to hold back water

force (FORS) pushing or pulling motion

foundations (foun-DAY-shuhnz) strong grounding

gravity (GRAV-ih-tee) force that attracts objects toward the center of the earth

notches (NAHCH-iz) indentations or cuts in an edge or surface

pressure (PRESH-ur) force that is produced when something presses or pushes against something else

redirect (ree-duh-REKT) to move in a different direction

reservoir (REZ-ur-vwahr) pool of water that is created

resist (rih-ZIST) to push away

waterproof (WAW-tur-proof) able to keep out water

FIND OUT MORE

BOOKS

Graham, Ian, and David Antram (illustrator). *You Wouldn't Want to Work on the Hoover Dam!* New York: Franklin Watts, 2012.

Latham, Donna, and Andrew Christensen (illustrator). *Canals and Dams: Investigate Feats of Engineering*. White River Junction, VT: Nomad Press, 2013.

Nagelhout, Ryan. *How Do Dams Work?* New York: PowerKids Press, 2016.

Spilsbury, Louise. *Dams and Hydropower.* New York: Rosen Central, 2012.

WEB SITES

Association of State Dam Safety Officials
http://www.damsafety.org
This site provides links with different information about dams, including history, purpose, and safety.

PBS—Building Big: Dams
www.pbs.org/wgbh/buildingbig/dam
This site explains basic information about dams and includes examples of dams.

INDEX

ABOUT THE AUTHOR

Dr. Virginia Loh-Hagan is an author, university professor, former classroom teacher, and curriculum designer. She lives close to the Lake Hodges Dam. She lives in San Diego with her very tall husband and very naughty dogs. To learn more about her, visit www.virginialoh.com.